This book belongs to

_____

This book is dedicated to my children - Mikey, Kobe, and Jojo.
Feel the fear and do it anyways.

Shy Ninja

By Mary Nhin

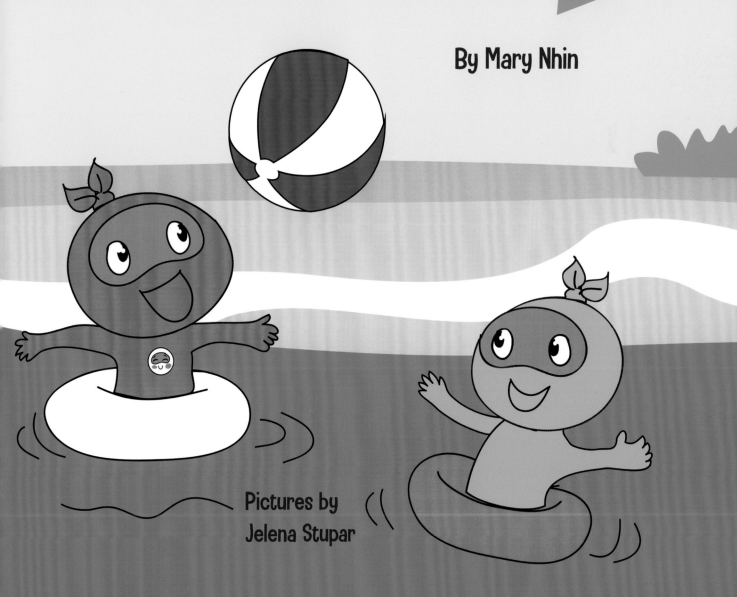

Pictures by
Jelena Stupar

I used to be really shy but now I'm not as shy...

At a party, I'd be the first to say "Hi," to you.

While waiting in line at the water fountain,
I'd give you a compliment.

And if you were the new kid on the soccer team,
I'd shake your hand to introduce myself.

If you didn't know me, you would have never known that I was once so shy it prevented me from doing things I loved to do.

When there was a game of four square going on,
I would be too embarrassed to ask to play.

Instead, I watched all the fun from a distance.

If I had a question to ask the teacher, I worried about asking in front of the whole class in case anyone laughed at me.

So after class, I would whisper my question.

And when it was time to perform my dance
routine, I felt scared that I might mess up.

So instead, I hid behind the curtain and missed my performance.

I was the shyest ninja of all until...

...I met Kind Ninja.

It was the first day of school.

And Kind Ninja could tell I was very nervous.

"Hey! There's no reason to feel worried. School's going to be a blast! I used to be kind of shy too until I I learned a strategy to calm my fears," said Kind Ninja.

I use the F.U.N. method:

Focus on breathing

Use positive self talk

Nudge fears aside

Next, use positive mantras.
And finally, nudge your fears aside.

As the bus neared the school, I began to think about what would happen on my first day of school.

My thoughts made me feel dizzy.

I could feel my face turn red, my heart race, and my palms sweat. I thought...

I focused on my breathing. I took a slow, deep breath, held it for 3 seconds, and then exhaled slowly. I did this 3 times.

Then, I used positive thoughts like *I can do this.*
Finally, I nudged my fears aside and exclaimed...

Move over fears, Shy Ninja is here!

And do you know what happened?

It worked!

For the first time ever, I felt confident that I could handle anything that came my way.

All I needed to do was focus on F.U.N.

Remembering the F.U.N. method could be your secret weapon against extreme shyness and social anxiety.

Focus

Use

Nudge

Please visit us at ninjalifehacks.tv for fun, free printables!!

⊡ @marynhin   @GrowGrit
#NinjaLifeHacks

f Mary Nhin   Ninja Life Hacks

▶ Ninja Life Hacks